LIFE IN THE TIME OF

AUGUSTUS

and the Ancient Romans

Michael Poulton

Illustrations by Christine Molan

RSVP
RAINTREE
STECK-VAUGHN
PUBLISHERS
The Steck-Vaughn Company

Austin, Texas

Published by Raintree Steck-Vaughn Publishers, an
imprint of Steck-Vaughn Company.

A Mirabel Book
Produced by Cynthia Parzych Publishing, Inc.
648 Broadway, N.Y., N.Y. 10012
Edited by: John Gilbert

Printed and bound in Belgium by Proost International
Book Production

1 2 3 4 5 6 7 8 9 0 Pl 98 97 96 95 94 93

Library of Congress Cataloging-in-Publication Data

Poulton, Michael.
    Life in the time of Augustus and the ancient
Romans / written by Michael Poulton; illustrated by
Christine Molan.
        p. cm. — (Life in the time of)
"A Mirabel book"—T.p. verso.
Includes index.
    Summary: Traces the rise to power of Gaius
Octavianus, later known as Augustus, and describes
life in the Roman empire during his reign.
    ISBN 0-8114-3350-1
    1. Rome—History—53-44 B.C.—Juvenile
literature. 2. Rome—History—Civil War, 43-31
B.C.—Juvenile literature. 3. Rome—History—Augus-
tus, 30 B.C.-14 A.D.—Juvenile literature. {1. Rome—
History—53-44 B.C. 2. Rome—History—Civil War,
43-31 B.C. 3. Rome—History—Augustus, 30 B.C.-14
A.D. 4. Rome—Social life and customs. 5. Augustus,
Emperor of Rome, 63 B.C.-14 A.D.} I. Molan,
Christine, ill. II. Title. III. Title: Augustus and the
ancient Romans. IV. Series.
DG269.P68 1993
937'.09—dc20
92-5824
CIP
    AC

For M. H.

COVER ILLUSTRATION:

Gaius Octavianus, the future Emperor Augustus, salutes
the crowd during Julius Caesar's victory parade.

PHOTO CREDITS:

Berlin Museum: 11 bottom
British Museum: 11 top, 12, 28 right, 30, 33, 44 top
Cassady, Richard: 60, 61
Centre National de la Recherche Scientifique, Paris: 45
Chang: Heidi: 46, 51
Connolly, Peter: 34
Germanisches Zentralmuseum, Mainz: 38
Gordon, Lucille: 26
Levin, Ira: 16, 27, 28 left, 57, 58
The Louvre, Paris: 15 top
Parzych, C.: 59
Rheinisches Landesmuseum, Bonn: 41

Contents

CHAPTER 1

Julius Caesar's Triumph

It is a public holiday in Rome. Everybody, rich or poor, aristocrat or slave, who has managed to slip away from his duties for an hour or two, is jostling for the best position on pavement, wall, or rooftop from which to watch the big parade. Julius Caesar, Rome's most powerful and popular general, is celebrating a victory.

At the head of the column march the senators and magistrates. They are followed by carts full of the treasures and armor captured from Caesar's enemies. Some carts have paintings that show the battles Caesar has won or models of the towns he has captured. Young men lead the white bulls, whose horns are gilded and necks hung with garlands, that are to be sacrificed at the Temple of Jupiter, chief of the gods, for this is really a religious procession. Some of the more important prisoners taken by Caesar are displayed, in chains, on pageant wagons. As the procession reaches the Sacred Way, a few of them are taken off to be executed.

Caesar now comes into view, standing in his great golden chariot pulled by a team of four white horses. Behind march the soldiers of his legions, carrying their standards and colors. They are wearing olive-leaf wreaths and shouting "Here comes the triumph!" to the excited crowd, who cheer wildly and toss flowers. Caesar is dressed in the robes of Jupiter, borrowed from the god's temple, yet he appears rather uncomfortable — a short, slightly built man who looks more like a clerk than a conqueror. He keeps a firm grip on the golden eagle scepter in his left hand, but the right hand, grasping an olive branch, is restless as he nervously smooths down his thinning hair. He inclines his head to hear what his charioteer is saying to him. He is deaf in one ear, and with all the noise, it is not easy to hear. Behind him in the chariot stands a slave who holds a crown of golden oak leaves a few inches above the general's head and every minute or so whispers something in his ear.

The Romans enjoy parades and like to honor their heroes. But they also believe in keeping them in their places. No matter how popular or powerful a man becomes, he is still a servant of the Roman state. The gods have a habit of knocking down those who climb too high. This is why the slave is riding beside the mighty conqueror. The warning words he whispers are "Remember you are only mortal." Unfortunately, he is whispering into Caesar's deaf ear.

WARNING SIGNS

Not everyone in the crowd is pleased that Caesar has grown so popular. Some of the patricians, or aristocrats, believe that he is planning to make himself king. The Romans dislike kings. They threw out the last one hundreds of years ago and set up a republic, governed by the Senate and people of Rome. But now, after years of civil war, the real power appears to be in the hands of the military leaders. As long as the generals fight among themselves, the Senate can play off one against the other. But if one of them comes out decisively on top, then anything may happen. And Caesar is almost on top.

The procession seems to go on for miles. It keeps stopping and starting as it winds its way through the streets. Toward the back come teams of comedians and clowns. They make jokes about Caesar and get the crowd laughing. The Romans do not seem to mind listening to scan-

The sixteen-year-old Gaius Octavianus is honored by his great-uncle Julius Caesar in the general's triumphal procession through Rome.

dalous songs on a solemn religious occasion. They like to be reminded that the heroes they set up as idols are only human and have faults and weaknesses in common with other men. Now Caesar's soldiers join in with bawdy songs — about his baldness, about the women he likes to chase, and about some of the outrageous things he did at wild parties given by King Nicomedes of Bithynia. Caesar may be deaf, but he senses the laughter in the crowd. He turns to glare at his soldiers, who look at the ground and snicker. They also have something else to smile about. Their general is looking rather odd today. According to custom, a victor celebrating a triumph has his face and arms painted bright red, and it takes some getting used to.

Caesar stiffens and stares straight ahead. Riding on one of the lead horses of the chariot is a handsome sixteen-year-old who seems to be getting almost as much attention from the crowd as Caesar. But Caesar does not mind. This is Gaius Octavianus, Caesar's sister's grandson. As the general has no children of his own, he is planning great things for the boy. But that lies in the future.

Suddenly, disaster! The axle of Caesar's chariot breaks. There are groans from the crowd.

A tense moment as Caesar, face painted red in celebration of his triumph, descends from his immobilized chariot. The masked actor at right circulates in the crowd to remind Caesar and his admirers that he is mortal and not a god.

On the steps of the Temple of Jupiter, Caesar prepares to crawl up the steps and preside over the sacrifice of a white bull.

The Romans are very superstitious people and clearly this is a bad omen. The thought crosses Caesar's mind that one of his many enemies may have planned the breakdown. But for now, something has to be done to ward off the bad luck. Everybody knows the story of the Roman admiral who was setting off for a big sea battle. His priests warned him not to fight, telling him that the sacred chickens were off their food — a very bad sign indeed. The admiral, impatient to engage the enemy, picked up the chicken coop and threw it into the sea. "If they won't eat, let 'em drink instead!" he sneered. The Roman fleet suffered one of its worst defeats in history.

Caesar steps down from the chariot and talks to the priests. They tell him that to set matters right he must crawl on his hands and knees up the steps of the Temple of Jupiter. Caesar flinches, but all eyes are upon him. He approaches the marble staircase, drops to the ground, and begins to crawl upward.

Things go better after this. At last he stands in front of the marble altar and faces the crowd. The boys lead the first white bull forward and remove its garlands. Caesar covers the animal's head, offers the appropriate prayers to Jupiter, then watches the ax smash down on its neck. The bad luck has been averted. All may yet be well.

ABOVE: A bust of Julius Caesar in his prime. TOP: Scene from a stone frieze depicting a bull being led to sacrifice.

CHAPTER 2

Caesar's Heir

On the morning of March 15, 44 B.C., Julius Caesar, now dictator, set off for a meeting of the Senate. The Senate building was closed for repair, so the meeting was to be held in a theater built by Caesar's dead rival, Pompey. As Caesar climbed the steps to the theater, he was handed a letter. He did not bother to read it. The letter warned him of his coming assassination. Minutes later, he was lying dead at the foot of Pompey's statue, stabbed repeatedly with daggers and the steel pens that the senators used for writing notes. The assassins, led by the senators Brutus and Cassius, rushed out of the theater shouting "freedom" and "liberty," and all the other slogans assassins usually shout. Inside the theater, amid the confusion, nobody seemed to know what to do next. Many people were pleased by Caesar's death, but none dared make any move until they saw how the people of Rome reacted. The statesman and well-known bore Cicero, who usually had an answer for everything, had not attended the meeting. It was probable he had known about the plot and kept well away. The consul Marcus Antonius, Caesar's friend and second in command, was nowhere to be found. Had the assassins killed him, too?

Three hundred miles to the east, across the sea in Macedonia, northern Greece, Gaius Octavianus, now eighteen, was completing his military training and perfecting his knowledge of Greek. He had spent much of his life on his rich stepfather's country estate at Vellitrae,

Coin with design of daggers to commemorate the assassination of Julius Caesar.

25 miles south of Rome. Unusually, his mother had taken care to provide him with an excellent education.

After leading a sheltered life, Octavian seemed more at home with simple country people than with the politicians and army officers in Rome. Of course, he knew all about Julius Caesar, his mother's famous uncle. Octavian was probably sixteen before he met Caesar — and then his outlook changed rapidly.

Caesar had Octavian elected to the college of priests and offered to take the boy to the wars he was planning in Africa. But Octavian's mother would not let him go. When Caesar returned victorious from the war, he included Octavian in his triumphal procession, raised him to the aristocracy, gave him a number of public duties to perform, and invited him to Spain to fight another war. Octavian was so excited that he became ill. Once again, the great general set off without him. When he recovered, Octavian sailed for Spain, only to be shipwrecked on the enemy coast. He managed to escape capture and slipped through the enemy lines into Caesar's headquarters. He received a very warm welcome from his famous relative.

Caesar's next big war would be against Parthia. Today this land includes parts of Iraq and Iran. Octavian accompanied six legions to Macedonia to prepare for war, while Caesar returned to Rome. The boy was given the position of master of the horse — it was rather like

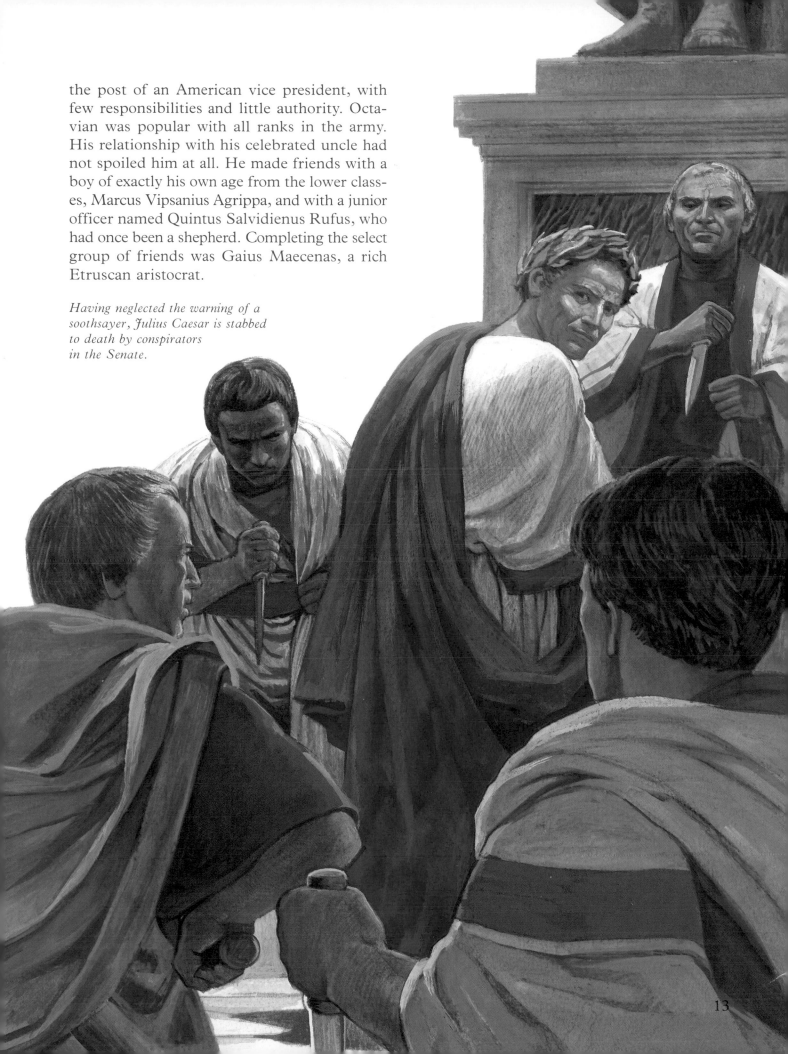

the post of an American vice president, with few responsibilities and little authority. Octavian was popular with all ranks in the army. His relationship with his celebrated uncle had not spoiled him at all. He made friends with a boy of exactly his own age from the lower classes, Marcus Vipsanius Agrippa, and with a junior officer named Quintus Salvidienus Rufus, who had once been a shepherd. Completing the select group of friends was Gaius Maecenas, a rich Etruscan aristocrat.

Having neglected the warning of a soothsayer, Julius Caesar is stabbed to death by conspirators in the Senate.

13

Sea journeys in the Mediterranean frequently carried risks. Young Octavian sailing to Spain to join Caesar's armies, was shipwrecked on the enemy coast.

Octavian had been living in the town of Apollonia for about three months, expecting his uncle to arrive any day. Instead, he received a letter from his mother, informing him that the general had been assassinated by a powerful group of senators, that he himself was in great danger, and that he should return home at once and trust nobody.

When the commanders of Caesar's Macedonian legions learned of their leader's death, they were angry and offered to depart for Italy under Octavian's command to bring the killers to justice. Agrippa and Salvidienus were eager to adopt this course of action, but Octavian was more cautious. To move the legions back into Italy would take weeks of planning, and nobody knew the strength of Brutus, Cassius, and their followers. Nor was there any news of Caesar's old friend, Marcus Antonius. He should have been organizing supporters of the dead Caesar. Some said that Antonius had been jealous of the influence Octavian had over his great-uncle. Had the assassins murdered Antonius as well? Perhaps he had made peace with them. Or maybe he was just lying low, drunk and incapable. Anything was possible with the unstable, unpredictable Marcus Antonius.

Octavian and a handful of friends sailed back across the Adriatic, avoiding the great port of Brundisium, where he thought the assassins might be lying in wait. They need not have worried. Brutus, Cassius, Antonius, and the others had not given them a minute's thought. They had far more pressing problems, and there could be no possible threat from an eighteen-year-old, far away at school in Greece. Octavian and his friends did not know this. They put ashore unseen a few miles south of the port. Nervously, they walked into the nearest small town and inquired about the news from Rome. The news was disturbing but also exciting. Marcus Antonius had sent offers of peace to the assassins, but then the citizens of Rome had taken matters into their own hands. After giving Caesar a great public cremation in the Forum, they had run riot. They had chased the assassins out of Rome, killed some of them, and burned their houses. Caesar's will had then been read in public. He had left his citizens a great deal of money and an inheritance to two of Octavian's cousins. But Octavian, now to be recognized as Caesar's adopted son, would inherit the largest part of Caesar's vast fortune.

The little group decided to risk walking to Brundisium. Here two letters awaited Octavian. The first, from his mother, ordered him home immediately. The second, from his stepfather, advised him to stay away from the upheaval in Rome, not to accept his inheritance, nor the adoption, but to lie low and be content with a private life. An almost unknown eighteen-year-old with no real military experience and no knowledge of politics was simply asking for trouble if he involved himself in public affairs in any way. Octavian did go home. But he told his parents that he would accept the inheritance and the adoption. From now on his friends were to call him by his new name: Gaius Julius Caesar. Moreover, he announced he would go to Rome.

CHAPTER 3

Octavian Goes to Rome

As Octavian and his friends slowly made their way to Rome, they were welcomed everywhere by Julius Caesar's soldiers, who pledged their support. In Rome there was a rather uneasy truce. Marcus Antonius had the support of most of the citizens and some of Caesar's legions. He was

CHRONOLOGY

These are the main events in the life of Augustus:

B.C.

63	Birth of Octavian, probably in Rome.
44	Murder of Julius Caesar (March) in the Theater of Pompey.
43	Octavian consul for the first time.
42	Battle of Philippi. Deaths of Brutus and Cassius.
39	Mark Antony marries Octavia.
38	Octavian marries Livia.
36	Defeat and execution of Sextus Pompeius. Lepidus sacked.
31	Battle of Actium.
30	Deaths of Antony and Cleopatra.
29	Octavian celebrates his first triumph.
27	Octavian receives title of Augustus.
20	War in Armenia. Treaty with Parthian Empire.
17	Ludi Saeculares (Secular Games) celebrated.
12	Death of Agrippa. Livia's son Tiberius compelled to divorce his wife and marry Julia.
8	Death of Maecenas.
5	Tiberius retires to Rhodes.
2	Augustus named Pater Patriae " Father of his Country" by Senate. Julia, Augustus' daughter, disgraced.

A.D.

2	Death of Augustus' grandson Lucius. Tiberius returns to Rome.
4	Death of Augustus' other grandson Caius. Augustus adopts Tiberius.
9	Three legions, under command of P. Quintilius Varus, destroyed by Germans in the Teutoburger Forest.
14	Death of Augustus at Nola in Campania.

Gold coin depicting the young Emperor Augustus.

Detail from a sarcophagus showing a boy being educated by his father in the art of rhetoric or public speaking.

also consul — joint leader of the Senate. He ought to have been in a position to take control.

Yet many of the aristocrats supported the murderers. Caesar had treated them as if they were his subjects. Brutus and Cassius might have been chased out of the city, but they, too, had legions to support them. The cunning statesman Cicero tried to play off the two groups against each other. He saw the death of the dictator as a chance to restore the power of the Senate. The last thing he wanted was for Marcus Antonius to inherit Caesar's popularity and power. Nobody gave much thought to the schoolboy who now called himself Gaius Julius Caesar.

OCTAVIAN MEETS ANTONIUS

Octavian might have expected a welcome from his great-uncle's old friend, but Antonius treated him very coldly and asked him bluntly what he wanted. Octavian replied that he had decided to accept the adoption and that he wanted the courts to recognize his claim. He explained that he had taken possession of Caesar's house and other properties, but that the vast amount of money he had been left, plus all his great-uncle's papers, were missing. Octavian needed the money at once as Caesar had left every citizen a cash gift in his will, and he intended to honor the wishes of his "father." In those days, there were no such things as bank vaults and checkbooks. Money existed in coins of gold and silver. Large sums, such as wages for the army, had to be carted around the country under heavy guard. Some of the safest places in Rome were its temples. Octavian had heard that Caesar's money had been kept in the Temple of Ops and that Antonius had taken it away.

Columns of the Temple of Castor and Pollux in the Roman Forum. In addition to being places of worship, temples were often used to safeguard money and valuables.

Antonius began to shout and threaten. He claimed that Julius Caesar had been almost bankrupt when he died. What little money he left belonged to the state. How dare anybody suggest that Marcus Antonius would cheat a boy out of his inheritance?

It is very probable that Antonius had used the money to pay his soldiers. Nobody can be sure. What is certain is that very little remained.

WINNING POPULAR SUPPORT

Octavian had money of his own, and he enjoyed the backing of many of Caesar's rich friends and soldiers. What he needed was publicity and popularity. So he decided to turn the affair of the missing cash to his own advantage. He let it be known that he had received none of the money left to him in the will, but even so he was prepared to pay the Roman citizens what his "father" had promised them. He began to hold public auctions of some of Caesar's property and possessions in order to raise the necessary cash. Antonius was furious.

Next Octavian announced that he would go ahead with the series of games that Julius Caesar had been planning in honor of the goddess Venus, whom he claimed was a distant ancestor. The people of Rome loved such gladiatorial games. They enjoyed watching combatants kill each other in the circus ring. Today we take similar pleasure in watching violent films in which people are blown to bits. The only difference is that in Roman times the deaths were real. Gladiatorial games were vastly expensive to stage. And, just as individuals and companies nowadays pour money into sponsorship, so Romans who wished to become popular with the citizens spent fortunes on the games.

On the opening evening of the games sponsored by Octavian, a comet was seen in the northern sky and reappeared every night for a week. Octavian wrote: "Everybody believed that the comet was a sign in the heavens that the soul of Caesar had gone to join the immortal gods. Because of this, a star was attached to the head of the statue of Caesar which, soon after, I unveiled in the Forum." Privately, he did not

The comet that appeared nightly for a week was seen by Octavian as a sign that the gods were protecting and favoring him.

BATTLE FOR POWER

As Antonius began to march toward Rome, his support gradually melted away. Three of his legions deserted to Octavian. All Antonius could do was to march his remaining army into Cisalpine Gaul in northern Italy and await developments. Even here he did not feel safe. The province of Cisalpine Gaul was occupied by Decimus Brutus, one of the conspirators against Caesar. Brutus and his army did not feel strong enough to fight Antonius, so they shut themselves up in the town of Mutina and prepared for a siege. Back in Rome, the Senate declared their support for Decimus Brutus and ordered Antonius to return to Rome without his army. He refused.

Cicero wanted to send help to Brutus in Mutina. But the Senate had no army in Italy to call upon. The only person with any forces under his command was Octavian, who had managed to raise five legions from the ranks of Caesar's best soldiers. The Senate had made a complete fiasco of their dealings, first with the assassins, then with Antonius. Now they would have to ask a nineteen-year-old schoolboy to defend the Republic for them. Cicero thought he could influence and manipulate Octavian and his supporters. He remarked jokingly to his friends that the boy should be flattered, raised to great heights, and then dropped. Octavian was made a senator and it was agreed that a statue of him on horseback should be erected in the city. Two new consuls, Aulus Hirtius and Vibius Pansa, took office on the first day of January, and the Senate decided that they, together with Octavian, should restore order in the north.

There were a number of skirmishes and two full battles. The first, at Forum Gallorum, was very bloody. Antonius was forced to retreat, but the consul Pansa was fatally wounded. Two weeks later, there was a second battle, under the walls of Mutina. The consul Hirtius was killed, but by this time Antonius' army was smashed. He retired to southern Gaul with the remains of his legions. In Gaul he hoped to raise more men and join forces with another of Caesar's old friends, Lepidus, now governor of Gaul.

share the popular view. He told his friends that the star was born for him; it was a sign that his fortunes were protected by the gods. Antonius, angered again, began to be alarmed by the public support for Octavian. He was also being attacked in the Senate by Cicero and his friends.

Caesar's veteran soldiers could not understand why Caesar's friend should treat the general's "son" so badly. They arranged a public meeting and made the two swear to be friends. This was not enough for Antonius. He felt he needed more military support. He ordered the six legions from Macedonia to cross back into Italy and land at Brundisium. Cicero was worried that Antonius would march the legions on Rome and take absolute power by force. But while Cicero stayed at home and worried, Octavian acted. With a small group of friends, including Agrippa and Maecenas, he moved south, taking with him several cartloads of money and pamphlets pleading his cause. He hoped to raise a small army from Caesar's supporters and win over the Macedonian legions to his side.

Octavian had served his purpose. The Senate decided to be firm with him in case he became too big for his boots. It awarded the Mutina battle honors to Decimus Brutus. Cicero, trying to appease everybody, proposed at least giving Octavian an ovation — a victory parade rather less grand than a triumph. However, the Senate had no wish to see the son of the dead dictator publicly idolized and rejected the motion. Octavian must have smarted under the insult.

Decimus Brutus was ordered to follow Anto-nius and destroy him. Octavian was instructed to hand over two of his Macedonian legions to Brutus. Letters were sent to Lepidus in Gaul ordering him to support Brutus against Antonius.

Caesar's assassins now had the support of the Senate. Marcus Brutus had disobeyed the Senate's orders and taken his armies into northern Greece. Despite this, the Senate made him governor of Macedonia and Illyricum. Cassius had occupied Syria with his legions. Now the Senate decided to legalize the occupation. It was beginning to look as if, by fighting against

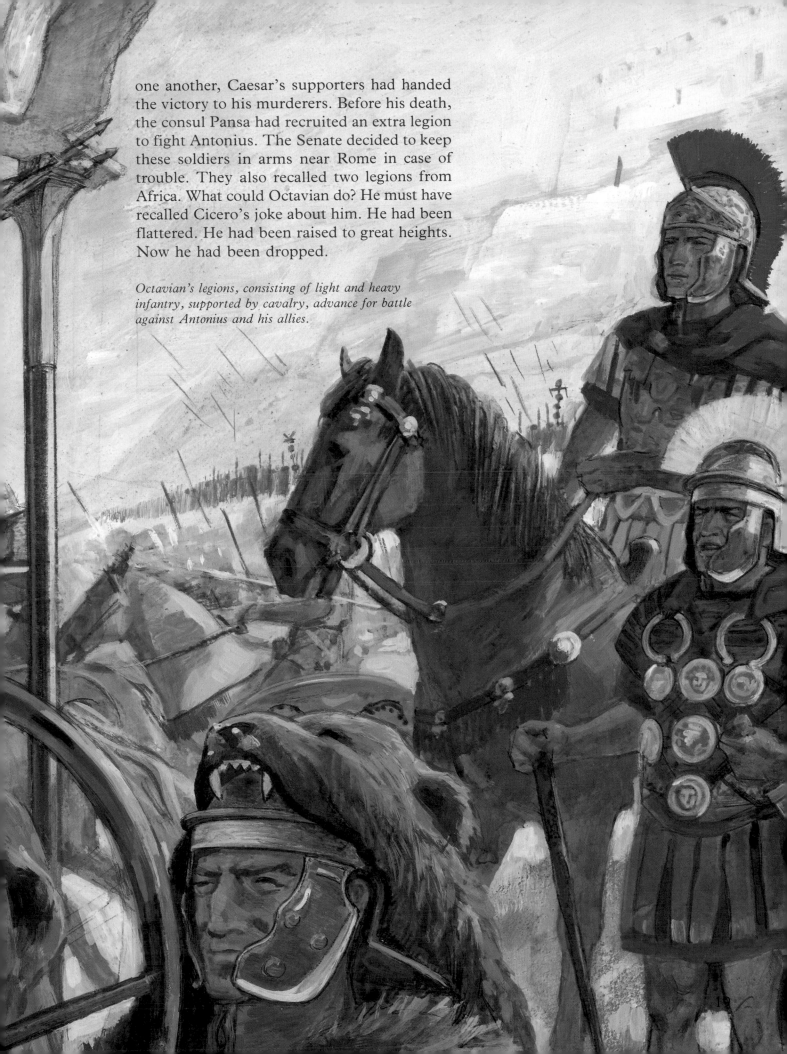

one another, Caesar's supporters had handed the victory to his murderers. Before his death, the consul Pansa had recruited an extra legion to fight Antonius. The Senate decided to keep these soldiers in arms near Rome in case of trouble. They also recalled two legions from Africa. What could Octavian do? He must have recalled Cicero's joke about him. He had been flattered. He had been raised to great heights. Now he had been dropped.

Octavian's legions, consisting of light and heavy infantry, supported by cavalry, advance for battle against Antonius and his allies.

CHAPTER 4

Octavian and Antonius

Octavian wrote to the Senate, pointing out that he could not lend two legions to Decimus Brutus because his soldiers refused to serve under a man who had supported Caesar's murder. He also said that he wanted to be made consul. There were laws preventing anyone as young as Octavian from taking such a high office. Octavian suggested the law be changed. He sent 400 of his most experienced centurions to Rome to argue his claim for the consulship. The Senate ignored them. Cicero wrote to Marcus Brutus in Macedonia, confidently claiming to have squashed the young man's ambitions.

Octavian and his legions began to march on Rome. At first the Senate flew into a panic. There was not time to get help from Marcus Brutus or Cassius, nor even Lepidus. Decimus Brutus was supposed to be dealing with Antonius. Some of them proposed that Octavian be given what he wanted. Then they realized that they still had Pansa's legion in Rome and that the two legions from Africa were due to arrive any day. They sent Octavian angry letters. Almost immediately came the biggest blow of all. The legion in Rome and the two from Africa had joined Octavian and were backing his claim. The young man, full of confidence, entered the city.

At a meeting of the Senate, Cicero arrived late. Octavian smiled and greeted him with the words, "Ah, here comes the last of all my friends!" The Senate made Octavian and one of his cousins consuls for the year and passed a law condemning to death *in absentia* Marcus Brutus, Gaius Cassius, and the rest of the assassins. Octavian took over the treasury and paid his soldiers well for their support. Decimus Brutus decided to join Marcus Brutus in Macedonia, but his legions deserted, some to Antonius, some to Octavian; he was murdered by a Gaulish chieftain while trying to escape.

Now the soldiers in the legions of Antonius and Octavian took a hand in the affair. They decided that it was time for the two generals to settle their differences. They were all Julius Caesar's men. Why should they squabble among themselves while Caesar's murderers went free?

LEFT: Fulvia, Antonius' wife, was one of the few women in Rome who had a position of power and influence.
RIGHT OPPOSITE: The triumvirs, Octavian, Antonius, and Lepidus, meet on an island and agree to share power.

RALLYING THE FORCES

Octavian, Antonius, and Lepidus met for a conference on a small island in a river in northern Italy. Here it was agreed that Octavian would resign his consulship, but the three of them would share absolute power as "triumvirs." A list was made of 130 senators, including Cicero, and a greater number of aristocrats who had aided Caesar's murderers. They were condemned to death, a reward was offered for their capture, and their property was confiscated by the state. It was also decreed that the dead Caesar was to be worshiped as a god. Octavian now could, and did, call himself "son of god."

Cicero was arrested trying to escape from his estate in southern Italy. His head was sent to Rome and nailed to a post. Antonius' wife, Fulvia, took a brooch from her dress and stuck the pin through the dead man's tongue, as if to say, "Now talk your way out of that!"

DAY OF RECKONING

The combined forces of Octavian and Antonius met those of Brutus and Cassius at Philippi in northeastern Greece. Two battles were fought, the first on October 23, 42 B.C., the other a few weeks later. After their defeat, both Brutus and Cassius committed suicide. Most of their influential supporters were killed in the fighting.

Antonius kept the larger part of the army and took over Rome's eastern provinces. Octavian returned to Rome. He had been given the difficult task of demobilizing the troops. That meant settling them in colonies and finding them land to farm. Unfortunately, there was not a great deal of land free in Italy. Octavian would have to buy what he could for his soldiers and confiscate the rest from towns that had not shown sufficient enthusiasm for his wars with the assassins. Perhaps Antonius hoped that the job would make the young man unpopular at home. Octavian carried out his duties fairly and efficiently and cemented the loyalty of his veteran soldiers.

The next few years brought other problems for the young man. Sextus Pompeius, son of Pompey the Great, Caesar's old enemy, seized the province of Sicily with a large fleet of ships and threatened Rome's trading routes. Much of the food Rome needed came from Africa. Sextus Pompeius could cut off the food supply and hold Rome to ransom. Lepidus, it was thought, was siding with Pompeius and had to be stripped of most of his power. Antonius' wife, the repulsive Fulvia, joined with Lucius, Antonius' brother, and led a revolt against Octavian. Slowly and patiently, Octavian dealt with these problems. But it was obvious to many people that the Roman world was not big enough to contain both Octavian and Antonius. Sooner or later there would be a war.

CHAPTER 5

Antonius and Cleopatra

Egypt was one of the richest countries in the Roman world. It was ruled by a Greek descendant of one of Alexander the Great's generals. Her name was Cleopatra. She had supported Julius Caesar in his wars against Pompey, and she claimed that Caesar was the father of her eldest son, whom she named Caesarion. Now she turned her attentions to Antonius and bore two children by him. Cleopatra was a very ambitious woman. She is believed to have boasted that she and Antonius could conquer the world. In Rome there was a story that she had said, "One day I shall make laws on the Capitol," meaning that she intended to rule the Romans. Antonius was firmly under her spell.

In patching up one of his many quarrels with Octavian in the years following Philippi, Antonius, a widower, had married Octavia, Octavian's favorite sister. Antonius had a reputation for the sort of debauched behavior — hard drinking, swearing, and pursuing women — that might even be frowned upon today. Octavia seemed to have tamed him. Octavia is one of the few people in Roman history for whom nobody has had a bad word. She was faithful, loyal, and patient, and possessed all the virtues the Romans admired. She and Antonius lived happily together in Athens for many years.

SEEDS OF WAR

In 37 B.C. Antonius sent Octavia back to her brother. He was about to fight a war against the Parthians and said she would be safer in Rome. But at the end of a long and disastrous campaign, he refused to recall his wife or even to answer her letters. At one point in the war she had personally taken him much-needed supplies for his army and 10,000 hand-picked soldiers. He refused her gifts and ordered her back to Rome.

The dress and jewelry of this noble woman in Roman Egypt illustrate the opulence of high society in this province of the empire.

He now married Cleopatra, although the Romans were forbidden by law to wed foreigners. He set up his headquarters at Alexandria in Egypt and proclaimed Cleopatra "Queen of Kings" and her son Caesarion "King of Kings."

To their own children he made gifts of entire kingdoms and announced that their eldest son, Alexander Helios — named after both Alexander the Great and the sun god — would have the whole Parthian Empire. Although, of course, he had not yet conquered Parthia, Antonius was confident that he would get around to it. Caesarion was also declared Julius Caesar's natural son and heir.

Octavian had no choice but to fight. The Romans were suspicious of foreigners, particularly of the Egyptians. Egypt, they believed, was the world center of depraved luxury, drunkenness, and other perversions. Rumors flew around

Rome that Antonius was planning to make Alexandria the capital of the Roman world. Such a decision would cause as much concern as if a modern American President were to propose moving Congress to Puerto Rico.

All the cities in Italy and all the towns in the western provinces swore an oath of loyalty to Octavian. Antonius' friends in Rome were permitted to leave and join him. Then Antonius' will was taken from the Temple of Vesta, where it had been deposited for safekeeping, and read to the Senate. It confirmed the Romans' worst suspicions. It said that Caesarion was Julius Caesar's true son and heir, that Cleopatra's children would inherit vast amounts of money and

23

The naval battle of Actium, off the west coast of
Greece, involved 900 warships and thousands of
infantry soldiers fighting at close quarters. Octavian
won a decisive victory over the forces of Antonius,
paving the way for his supreme power in Rome.

land, and if Antonius were to die away from Egypt, that his body should be sent to Cleopatra in Alexandria for burial there. This last disloyalty to Rome offended the citizens even more than all the other provisions in the will. Octavian could delay no longer and declared war on Cleopatra.

THE WAR

Antonius moved his legions into Greece. Octavian fortified the east coast of Italy. Octavian's old friend Agrippa, who had become his most trusted adviser and general, conducted a series of brilliant raids and cut Antonius' supply lines. Antonius had many more soldiers than Octavian, but most of them were suffering from hunger or malaria. Many deserted him.

The Battle of Actium was fought at sea. Shortly after it began, Cleopatra set sail and fled. Antonius followed her. Octavian captured 300 warships and destroyed the remainder of Antonius' fleet. Antonius' troops on land surrendered.

Octavian moved slowly toward Alexandria, handing out punishments to his enemies and rewards to his supporters on the way. Antonius stabbed himself and died in Cleopatra's arms. Most of all, Octavian wanted to capture Cleopatra alive so that he could display her in his triumph in Rome. When they met, Cleopatra used all her charm on him. It had worked with Julius Caesar, and it had worked with Antonius. But it failed to work with Octavian. She, too, killed herself. Octavian executed Caesarion and kept the kingdom of Egypt and all its wealth for his personal use. The

children of Antonius and Cleopatra were sent to Rome, where they were loved and cared for by the saintly Octavia.

Before leaving Alexandria, Octavian went to view the preserved body of Alexander the Great. When the lid was lifted from the sarcophagus, Octavian stared for some time at the face of the youthful conqueror. In touching the face, he slightly damaged the nose. The Egyptian priests asked him if he would also like to see the mummified bodies of the Egyptian pharaohs. Octavian replied, "I came to see a king, not a load of corpses."

The remains of a Roman temple, recently discovered in Alexandria, Egypt. Roman rule began after Cleopatra's suicide in 30 B.C. and lasted for nearly seven centuries.

26

CHAPTER 6

Religion

Statue of a Vestal Virgin in the Forum. The priestesses kept alight the eternal flame of Vesta, goddess of the hearth, whose shrine was the holiest religious shrine in Rome.

Having, as he said himself, "stamped out the civil wars," Octavian set about bringing peace and order to the Roman lands. He had a particular interest in religion. He saw it as the cement that would bind the Roman people together. First he proceeded to restore the many temples and religious rites that had been neglected during the civil war.

PRIESTS AND AUGURS

The chief priest in Rome was called the *Pontifex Maximus*. The name means something like a great bridge between the people and the gods. Octavian became chief priest. From then on the office was always held by the reigning emperor. Today the title Pontifex Maximus is held by the pope.

The Pontifex Maximus had two groups of advisers, the college of priests and the college of augurs. The priests were in charge of religion and religious ritual, but the priesthood was a public honor and duty rather than a full-time job. The augurs had the special task of determining the will of the gods. They looked at signs in the heavens, such as comets, thunder and lightning, or the flights of birds. They examined the entrails of sacrificed animals, then read the signs to find out what the gods wanted. Astrologers, by contrast, attempted to predict the future from the movement of the stars. Before a war or a battle, the augurs would try to see from the omens whether the gods would be on Rome's side. On a more humble level, a merchant might request an augur to read the omens before sending his ships on a trading journey. The ships would only set out on a lucky day. On the morning of March 15, 44 B.C., Julius Caesar had asked his augurs what sort of a day he would have. When they told him it was a very unlucky day for him, he decided to ignore their warning. It was the day of his assassination.

THE TEMPLE OF VESTA

The most sacred shrine in Rome was the Temple of Vesta, goddess of the hearth. Inside the shrine burned a sacred flame, a symbol of the Roman homeland, tended by its priestesses, the Vestal Virgins. Once a year, on New Year's Day, they extinguished the flame then relit it. This symbolized the return of light and heat to the world after the long winter. No man was allowed to observe these rites. Every five years a girl from the patrician class was elected to the college of priests. She would hold the office, one of Rome's highest honors, for thirty years. Like a nun, she was not permitted to marry. Eventually, Octavian was forced to open the priesthood to non-patrician girls because of the shortage of suitable volunteers. The temple was so sacred that it was considered one of the safest places in Rome. Octavian was severely criticized for forcing the Vestal Virgins to hand over Antonius' will.

THE GODS

All the chief Roman deities had at least one temple in Rome. They included Jupiter, chief of the gods; Mars, the war god; Neptune, god of the sea; Juno, chief of the goddesses; Venus, goddess of love; Apollo, god of wisdom and the sun; Mercury, the divine messenger, who, among other things, was god of thieves; Aesculapius, god of healing; Bacchus, god of wine; and many others. There were also many local divinities and others associated with particular professions or activities. The twins, Castor and Pollux, were the gods of horse racing and boxing. Vulcan was god of smiths.

Statue of Apollo, Greek god of the sun, of wisdom, of music and poetry, and of prophecy. The Romans adopted Apollo as one of their own divinities, and Augustus chose him as his personal god, building a temple to him on the Palatine Hill to celebrate the victory at Actium.

Ruins of the House of the Vestal Virgins, which adjoined the Temple of Vesta, in the Roman Forum.

Each of the gods and goddesses controlled some aspect of everyday life. A girl hoping for a happy marriage would sacrifice to Juno. A soldier going to war would sacrifice to Mars, a sailor to Neptune. The gods were believed to be in charge of people's luck or fortunes and so could be bribed: A sailor on a sinking ship might cry, "Get me out of this, Neptune, and I'll sacrifice a calf to you!" If it did not work, and he drowned, he would be in no position to blame the god for letting him down. A thief might offer part of the proceeds of his crime to Mercury. A sick person or someone with a broken leg or failing sight might sleep in the porch of the Temple of Aesculapius or perhaps leave a tiny model of a leg, or an eye, and a gift of money to the priests.

TEMPLES AND RITUALS

A temple was nothing like a modern church, synagogue, or mosque, nor did anything that we would recognize as a "service" take place there. Inside the temple was a huge statue of the god or goddess, poorly illuminated by flickering oil lamps. A citizen might stand in front of the statue to ask a favor and perhaps leave

Roman citizens invoked the blessing and favor of the gods by bringing them gifts. Women made offerings to Juno, the goddess who presided over marriage and childbirth.

an offering of money or a small statue to the god. Sometimes curses, inscribed on lead plates, were deposited in the shrine. A temple contained meeting rooms for the priests, a treasury for valuables (including robes and religious objects) and money, and perhaps a library.

Public rituals were held outside in the open air. Here, in front of the temple, or halfway up the steps, was the marble altar on which to sacrifice animals, and the charcoal-burning braziers on which to throw incense and the blood and guts of the sacrificial victims. Poorer people might sacrifice a rooster or a dove, richer folk a lamb, a ram, or a boar. The very wealthy might even sacrifice a whole herd of their best cattle. Wine offerings or "libations" were also often thrown into the flames. The smoke from the offerings, mingled with the incense, was thought to be pleasing to the gods.

The priest would cover his head with his robes. The boys who assisted him hung garlands of leaves, flowers, and ribbons on the animal and anointed it with precious oils and wine. Then they led it to the altar. A big animal was felled with an ax, a smaller one had its throat cut with a sacrificial knife. The augur examined the victim's intestines or sometimes its liver in order to read the omens. Members of the temple would then eat the best part of the meat.

THE TEMPLE OF MARS THE AVENGER

When he first came to Rome after the assassination of Julius Caesar, Octavian made a promise to Mars, god of war. He swore that if he destroyed Brutus, Cassius, and the other murderers in battle, he would build the god a new and splendid temple. The result was the Temple of Mars Ultor — Mars the Avenger. It stood in the new public square and marketplace that Octavian built for the people of Rome. It was not completed until the year A.D. 2, when Octavian was sixty-five years old.

All the Senate's war business was to be conducted from the new temple in the belief that here, in his sanctuary, Mars would be watching over the interests of the Roman people. The march to the place of war was to start from it. A commander who returned in triumph would deposit his victory crown and scepter in the temple. Many battle trophies were also placed there.

A magnificent series of games was held to celebrate the dedication of this temple. It includ-

29

THE TEMPLE OF APOLLO

In 36 B.C., Octavian's house on the Palatine Hill was struck by lightning. This was considered a very bad omen. To counter the bad luck, Octavian promised to build a splendid temple for Apollo, whom he regarded as a special protector. Because Octavian thought that the god had protected him during his wars with Antonius, he dedicated the temple to Apollo of Actium. Built on the Palatine Hill, it was surrounded by beautiful precincts and gardens. It had two libraries, one of Greek books, the other of Latin.

THE TEMPLE OF JULIUS CAESAR

The temples Octavian built were designed to glorify his achievements or his family. After the Senate, at his prompting, had made Julius Caesar a god, it was natural that Octavian should erect a temple to him. Octavian was clever enough

In the Circus Flaminius, under a huge canopy to give protection from sun and rain, the flooded arena is the setting for a savage crocodile hunt.
RIGHT: Detail of a stone relief showing women gladiators in an arena, an unusual scene.

ed the "Troy Game," a sort of battle on horseback between boys from Rome's leading families, horse races and gladiator fights, an animal hunt in the arena where 260 lions were killed, and a naval battle on a huge lake representing a rerun of the Athenian victory over the Persian fleet at Salamis. Real ships were used, and hundreds of people were killed. Once more the "Athenians" won. The Circus Flaminius was flooded for a crocodile hunt. The historian Dio Cassius tells us that thirty-six crocodiles were killed. He does not give the score for the other side.

to suggest to the Roman people that, although he himself was not a god, his ancestors, even by adoption, deserved to be worshiped.

THE PANTHEON

One of Rome's best preserved temples is the Pantheon. This circular temple was built by Agrippa, who dedicated it to Mars and Venus from whom, Julius Caesar claimed, the family was descended. Octavian, however, did allow images of himself and Agrippa to be placed in one of the temple's antechambers. In later centuries, the Pantheon was extended and rebuilt, and today the building is a Christian church.

THE LARES AND PENATES

The great gods of the Romans were for the most part imported from the Greeks. Zeus, "greatest and best," had probably originally come from India to Greece, then, as "father Zeus" or "Zeus pater" he became the "Jupiter" of the Romans.

Apollo, probably the most important of the gods, continued, his name unchanged, to speak to humans through his oracle at Delphi. Eventually he became disgusted with what was happening on earth and moved from Delphi, leaving no forwarding address.

But Romans were really a farming people. Their favorite and most trusted gods were the spirits of the earth, the woods, streams, and flocks, and those that came indoors to look after the hearth and home. These were the ancestors of the goblins, hobgoblins, pucks, pooks, fairies, and elves that became a part of British and later American folklore.

Every Roman home had its shrine. Often the shrine was built in the shape of a miniature temple. Here family prayers were said to Vesta, and to the Lares and Penates — the spirits who looked after the family. The Lares and Penates were represented by little statues placed in or near the family shrine. Another of their duties was to care for the family's dead ancestors. Sometimes a person's genius — a spirit rather like a guardian angel — was represented as a bronze snake.

EMPEROR WORSHIP

As soon as Octavian (or Augustus as he was then called) died, he was made a god. During his lifetime many people were prepared to worship him as such, and Augustus did not wish to offend the Romans. Although he was an emperor and the most powerful man in the world, he wanted to preserve the idea that he was not above the law of the Roman state. But many of the eastern people, including the Greeks and Egyptians, were used to thinking of great men as deities. To the Egyptians Augustus was a pharaoh, a king on earth and a god in heaven. Augustus compromised. The Romans could regard him as a protecting spirit, but they must not treat him in Rome as a god. On the other hand, those peoples elsewhere in the empire who were accustomed to making gods of their rulers, could be allowed to worship him.

FOREIGN CULTS

Rome was a great trading center and the most important capital city in the western world. People from almost every known country lived there. Roman life was based on slave labor, and slaves from other lands naturally brought their religious customs with them. The Roman legions were stationed abroad far and wide. Some of them were bound to become interested in the religions of the countries in which they served. Rome, therefore, became a center for many religions that its citizens found strange. Many were tolerated. Some were frowned upon.

ISIS AND SERAPIS

Two cults from Egypt which found a good deal of support were those of Isis, chief goddess of the Egyptians, and of Serapis, the bull god. When Antonius and Octavian joined together to fight the assassins, they had actually considered building a temple in Rome to Isis, whose followers believed in a happy life after death. Following the war with Cleopatra, Octavian showed less tolerance. While in Egypt, some of the priests of Serapis had asked him if he would care to make a sacrifice to the bull god. Octavian replied: "I always respect the gods, but I'm not in the habit of worshiping cattle." Romans were forbidden to worship these Egyptian gods within their own city limits.

THE DRUIDIC CULT

Some of the nobles from Gaul who had been granted Roman citizenship, as well as slaves from this land, followed the ancient Celtic religion. Its priests, called Druids, favored human sacrifice. The Druids had led a fanatical opposition to Julius Caesar's invasion of Gaul. It is hardly surprising that Augustus banned their cult. When, more than thirty years after Augustus' death, the Romans invaded Britain, they did everything they could to stamp out Druidism at its roots. They succeeded almost completely, although the mistletoe we hang up at Christmas is a custom of the Druids.

THE JEWS

The Jews had a unique religion and took their faith very seriously. Herod the Great, king of the Jews, was not a true Jew, for his father was an Arab. Herod spent years rebuilding Solomon's Temple in Jerusalem, probably the most magnificent temple in the world. He placed a Roman imperial eagle over its most holy sanctuary. The Jews were outraged. Their laws

forbade them to make images or statues of anyone or anything. But the eagle remained until Herod was on his deathbed.

Herod ruled another people, the Samaritans, who did not get along with the Jews. At one time he considered moving his capital from Jerusalem to the splendid city he had built in Samaria which he called Sebaste — the Greek name for Augustus. This city was dominated by a huge Temple of Augustus. Augustus did not object to the honor and visited the temple.

Augustus was very tolerant of the Jewish religion in his early years. He had Jewish friends and advisers, including Herod the Great, and he brought up two of Herod's children . He safeguarded the rights of the Jews, permitting them to keep the Sabbath and to send money home. Nor did he force Jews to serve as auxiliary soldiers in the Roman army. To protect the Roman people, he paid for sacrifices to be made twice a day to the Jewish god in his temple in Jerusalem. Later, however, Augustus fell out with Herod. Besides, the Jewish faith insisted that there was only one god. Augustus must have felt that this conflicted seriously with his own beliefs.

AFTER AUGUSTUS

Following the death of Augustus in A.D. 14, many more foreign cults found their way to Rome. The worship of Mithras, the bull slayer, came from the east. It was an all-male religion that became popular in the army. Rituals were held in shrines that resembled the cave in which Mithras had slain the bull. We know little about Mithras because his followers were very secretive about him, but they were certainly concerned with the struggles between light and darkness — good and evil. In many places where the legions were stationed, temples and statues of Mithras and the bull have been found. It is very frustrating for a historian to have plenty of archaeological evidence but no written authorities to help bring the cult to life. Perhaps somebody, some day, will find a Mithras "gospel." Until then, what is known is mostly guesswork.

Two hundred years later, another boy emperor, Heliogabalus, tried to force the people of Rome to worship an eastern sun god. He placed a statue of his god in the Temple of Vesta and officiated at its outlandish rites. He was soon assassinated by the angry Romans.

The religion that survived in Rome was Christianity. Jesus of Nazareth was born toward the end of Augustus' reign. At first, Christianity was tolerated in Rome, then it was banned. Later emperors tried to stamp it out. But in A.D. 312 Christianity became the official religion of the Roman Empire.

ABOVE: A statue of Mithras excavated from a temple in London.
BELOW: Captured prisoners, with their shields and armor, are shackled and carried in triumph on a litter to be offered as human sacrifices to the gods.

CHAPTER 7

Augustus and the Roman Army

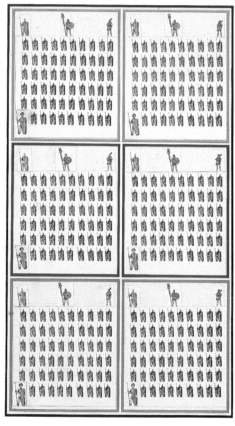

Diagram of Roman cohorts.

In January 27 B.C. Octavian was in a position of absolute authority. He said that he had decided to hand back the responsibility for governing Rome and its provinces to the Senate. When he announced his intentions, his words were greeted with carefully stage-managed protests from many of the senators. The Senate then passed a law that returned the real power to Octavian "that he may have the right and power to do whatever he shall judge to be in the best interests of the state." But Octavian objected that the responsibility was too great for him. Therefore a compromise was reached. Octavian kept control of most of the army and the provinces that were difficult to govern. He also kept a firm grip on the finances of the State. The Senate appeared to be in charge once more, but the truth was that they could make no important decisions without Octavian's consent.

ALL HONOR TO AUGUSTUS

Three days later, the senators met again. They wished to honor Octavian for saving Rome and restoring law and order. Dio Cassius says that they allowed Octavian to plant laurel trees in front of his house. He was also permitted to hang a wreath of oak leaves above his door — the highest reward for a great achievement. In addition, they decided that a golden shield should be hung in the Senate House, on which was to be engraved a list of Octavian's virtues: clemency, valor, justice, and piety. The Senate had once granted Julius Caesar the honor of allowing him to wear a laurel wreath at all times. This had delighted the dictator more than anything, for it helped to disguise his baldness.

They now gave Octavian a new name. From now on he was to be called Augustus, a title that suggested an almost sacred authority. In fact, Octavian was a little disappointed with his new name. He had let it be known that he would like to be called Romulus, after the man who was supposed to have founded Rome. The Senate, however, decided that Romulus was an unlucky name. Legend had it that Romulus had made himself king, had killed his brother, Remus, and had been assassinated in the Senate House.

THE ARMY

Augustus knew that the real power lay with the army, and he took great care to keep his soldiers happy. He was never much of a commander in battle, but his friend Agrippa had developed into something of a military genius.

Cohorts of the Praetorian Guard formed Augustus'
imperial bodyguard, performing ceremonial duties
as well as seeing active service.

Augustus had the good sense to trust Agrippa's advice in matters of war.

After the Battle of Actium, Augustus had more than fifty legions under his command. He disbanded almost half of them in the customary way — giving them grants of money or land. But he chose the twenty-eight best legions from his own and Antonius' forces and kept them as a standing army.

There were three main divisions in Augustus' army. These were the Praetorian Guard, the legions, and the *Auxilia*.

THE PRAETORIAN GUARD

It was usual for army commanders to have a bodyguard during times of war. Augustus, after Actium, retained his own guard as a large elite force. There were nine cohorts, each consisting of 1,000 men, of the best soldiers from Rome and the rest of Italy. Augustus kept one third of his guard in Rome and the rest in towns nearby. The praetorians were given special privileges to ensure their absolute loyalty. They had to sign up for a period of twelve years, which was a much shorter term than that of the ordinary soldier, and their pay was considerably better. At the end of Augustus' reign they were paid three times more than was a common soldier.

It was also usual for a general to keep a small bodyguard of foreigners. Augustus' troop were Germans, who spoke their own language and did not mix with other units. Since they depended for everything upon the emperor, their loyalty was absolute. Antonius had kept a bodyguard of Gauls which he gave to Cleopatra. After her death, Augustus handed them over to Herod the Great. The historian Josephus tells us that Herod once made his Gauls "accidentally" drown his seventeen-year-old brother-in-law, whom he had just appointed high priest, in the swimming pool of his palace at Jericho.

THE LEGIONS

In the earliest days of Rome, the legions had been made up of ordinary citizens who were mobilized to defend Rome whenever it was necessary. They were commanded in battle by the consuls and were loyal to the Senate. At the end of a campaign they went back to farming the land.

As Rome began to fight longer wars and win territories farther from home, it became impossible to manage military affairs on a voluntary basis. In the days before Julius Caesar came to power, generals started to recruit and pay professional soldiers. Signing up for twenty years, they would be well trained and generously paid. At the end of their army career, they could expect from their general a large cash payment or a grant of land. There were other changes. A soldier's first loyalty was now to the general who looked after him rather than to the Senate. His duties, too, began to alter. He had to become something of an engineer and builder as well as a fighting man. Roads, forts, walls, and aqueducts were all built by the army.

Legions were supposed to be made up of Roman citizens. Such citizens were not just the people who lived in Rome. They might come, for example, from other towns in Italy, most of which had been granted Roman citizenship, and they would enjoy similar rights and privileges. In the ranks of the twenty-eight legions that Augustus retained after Actium, there were many exceptions. The western legions mostly consisted of Italian recruits, but in the eastern legions there were very few. The foreigners in the eastern legions were allowed to adopt Roman names and were treated as citizens.

The majority of Augustus' legions had names and numbers. The numbers were not very helpful because they were often duplicated. For example, Augustus retained his own tenth legion and Antonius' tenth as well. There were two fourth, two fifth, and two sixth legions. And there were three third legions, which suggests that one of them must have been taken from

Herod murdered his wife, her brother (by drowning), her mother, her grandfather, and her two sons.

Lepidus. The names were sometimes official titles like II Augusta and III Augusta. Or they might come from places where they had served well, such as IV Macedonia or III Gallica. Others were nicknames, like the legion of Gauls enlisted by Julius Caesar known as *Alaudae* — "The Larks." Some of the legions that Augustus built up survived for a very long time indeed. Of the original twenty-eight, sixteen were in existence more than 400 years later. Others were not so lucky. Near the end of Augustus' reign, three legions were ambushed in the German forests and massacred.

Each legion was commanded by a legate, usually a senator in his early thirties. Under him served six junior officers called tribunes. The senior of the six was the second-in-command to the legate. The other five were normally young men who were learning the arts of war and did not possess much real authority. Third-in-command was the camp prefect, who was in charge of the day-to-day running of the legion. He supervised the building of the fortified camps, the engineering works, the supplies, and the equipment.

COHORTS AND CENTURIES

Every legion was divided into ten cohorts, each containing about 500 men. A cohort was further divided into six groups of eighty men called centuries. A century was made up of ten eight-man units who shared a tent and messed together. Each unit was known as a *contubernium*.

The century was commanded by a centurion and his *optio* or deputy. The senior centurion of the first cohort was the senior centurion of the whole legion. The legate would often turn to this group of officers for advice. The centurions were responsible for the discipline, training, and efficiency of the soldiers under their command. They carried a vine staff as their symbol of authority and would often use it to flog their men with great relish. There were frequent complaints about the brutality of the centurions. In battle, however, things changed. Most centurions would lay down their lives for their men and often did.

The legionaries followed their standard-bearers into battle. The main standard was an eagle, carried by an officer known as the *aquilifer*. The eagle was the legion's most sacred object. Unless the whole legion was engaged in a battle, the eagle would not leave its shrine at headquar-

A provincial legate (left),
a centurion (right),
and a legionary (below).

ters. On the field, it was guarded by the senior centurion and the first cohort. A legion could suffer no worse disgrace than lose an eagle in battle. In his memoirs, Julius Caesar tells a story about the expedition to Britain. His legions were aboard ship in the English Channel worrying about the Celtic tribesmen who lined the shore. However, nobody seemed eager to start the attack. The *aquilifer* of one of the legions picked up the eagle and jumped overboard shouting, "Follow me, men! Do you want to lose your eagle? I for one know my duty to my country and my general!" More probably he just yelled, "Come on, men!" but Caesar knew how to improve an incident into a good story, particularly if he had a role in it.

Each century had its own standard, carried by a *signifer*; and there were flags called *vexilla*, carried by a *vexillarius*, usually for raiding par-

Part of a Roman legionary's discharge diploma from Lebanon.

ties away from the main body of the legion. Later, there were standards with portraits of the emperor, carried by an *imaginifer*. Standard-bearers had other duties, too, such as looking after the legion's savings, its burial club money, and the sums collected by the men toward celebrating the twelve-day feast of the god Saturn called Saturnalia — the counterpart of today's Christmas. Close behind the standard-bearers were the trumpeters, who blasted out signals in battle.

THE PROFESSIONAL SOLDIER

The ordinary legionary signed up for sixteen years. Toward the end of his reign, Augustus raised this term to twenty years. The cost of his food, clothes, boots, weapons, and even his tent, were deducted from the soldier's pay. Even so, the rewards were considerable. A careful man could manage to save about a third of his wages. There were extra "perks," too. A general might pay a bonus after a victory, or a new emperor might make a special payment to the army to ensure the men's loyalty. After completion of his service, a soldier could expect a discharge payment in land or money worth about thirteen years' wages.

Soldiers kept themselves in the peak of physical condition with very tough training and daily drill, using blunt weapons and shields that were twice as heavy as real ones. A recruit was taught to fight, ride, and swim. Three times a month he had to go on a day's fast march for 20 miles, carrying equipment weighing over 90 pounds. At the end of it, he would have to help build a fortified camp.

During his time in the army, a soldier was

Map of the Roman Empire at the death of Augustus (A.D. 14).

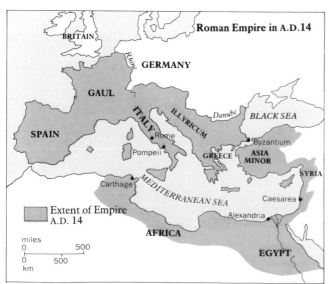

not allowed to marry. A married man who enlisted was automatically divorced. Augustus did not want women around to interfere with the serious business of soldiering. In places where a legion was stationed for many years, this was a very difficult rule to enforce.

Roman law said that the father was head of the family. Everything his children owned or earned belonged to him. This was very hard on a man who had joined the army to make his fortune. Augustus passed a law ruling that anything a soldier earned, and his share of any plunder, belonged to him. At one time, if a soldier died, his money would automatically go to his father. Augustus decided that a soldier had the right to make a will and leave his money to whomever he liked.

THE AUXILIA

The Roman army had always made use of foreign soldiers from their dependent kingdoms and the provinces. These auxiliary soldiers had their own special fighting skills and could do things that the regular legionary was not able to. In battle, for example, the Romans were never outstanding horsemen. The Auxilia provided the cavalry from countries such as Numidia, Gaul, and Spain. Syria produced archers, and Crete sent soldiers who were expert with slingshots. A Roman general would normally call up these allied forces at the beginning of a campaign and send them home as soon as hostilities were over. Augustus made the Auxilia a permanent part of his army. It was organized in exactly the same way as the regular legions. Originally men had been led by their own tribal chiefs, but by the time of Augustus they were usually commanded by military tribunes. Often the Auxilia opened a battle while the legions were held in reserve. It must have been dispiriting for an enemy to have to fight legions of auxiliaries, knowing that there were the same number of veteran soldiers behind the lines, waiting patiently to join in.

Legionaries on maneuvers dig an encampment, comprising earthworks and a surrounding palisade.

THE TEUTOBURGER FOREST
DISASTER

Augustus had inherited a vast empire. He spent the early part of his reign completing the conquests others had started. An immense area south of the Danube River was brought under Roman control. But Augustus was involved during most of his reign in keeping his lands secure and well fortified. He had no great ambitions to expand them further. Germany, however, was a problem. The Rhine River formed one of the borders of the empire. The Romans worried about raids by German tribesmen across the river and decided to occupy the far bank.

A Roman governor named Varus had become quite friendly with a local German chief named

Varus and his legions are ambushed in the Teutoburger Forest and wiped out by the Germans led by Arminius.

Arminius, or "Herman." In A.D. 9 news came of a revolt deep in Germany, beyond the lands occupied by Herman's tribe. Varus immediately set off with three legions, accompanied by Herman and his men, to restore order. Varus had no fears for his safety as he believed he was on friendly territory. After a while, however, Herman and his men said farewell to Varus and slipped away into the woods. Soon Varus found himself in serious difficulties. The land was mountainous and deeply forested. It began to pour with rain. The horsemen and the baggage train could hardly move through the thickly clustered trees.

The Germans began to fell trees across the muddy paths making progress even more difficult for the Romans. Then they began to hurl spears at the slowly moving column. Varus finally realized that he had been betrayed and trapped. The German raids became even more daring. Varus' men were used to fighting in the open. They tried to make a stand, but it was hopeless. Varus and his officers fell on their own swords, and three entire legions were wiped out.

When news reached Rome, Augustus, now an old man, tore his clothes and, in great distress, wandered around the palace crying, "Give me back my legions! Give me back my legions!" For a while he feared that the Germans might actually invade Italy, and he began to conscript young men into the army. Tiberius, Augustus' stepson, managed to regroup and restore order on the Rhine, but it was not until six years later, a year after Augustus died, that a Roman army dared advance into the Teutoburger Forest to find thousands of headless corpses still lying where they had fallen.

The tombstone of the centurion Marcus Caelius.

MARCUS CAELIUS, CENTURION OF THE XVIII LEGION

Historians know the name of one centurion who died, aged fifty-three, in the massacre in the German forest. This memorial illustrated in the photograph above, showing Marcus Caelius and his servants, was put up by his brother, Publius. It was discovered at Xanten on the Rhine. It was clearly a monument rather than a gravestone because the Romans buried the victims of the disaster in mass graves. Caelius is holding his centurion's vine staff. The ornaments on his breastplate are awards for bravery. They would be made of silver inlaid with gold. The round circular ornaments, called *phalerae,* are decorated with the heads of gods. On his shoulders are torques, which look like the gold ornaments worn on the wrists and neck by Celtic chiefs. On Caelius' wrists are thick bracelets, called *armillae.* On his head is a *corona civica,* a crown of oak leaves, a high honor awarded to a soldier who saved a companion's life at great risk to his own.

Ships and Trade

The wealth of an empire depends upon its trade. Rome was a great trading center. Into its port at Ostia, where the Tiber River flows into the sea, came the provisions needed to feed its growing population. Huge transport ships brought corn from Egypt and other parts of Africa. Some could carry more than 1,000 tons. Smaller vessels kept Rome well supplied with fish, olive oil, and wine. Luxury goods arrived from all over the empire and even farther afield. By the time of Augustus, 120 ships a year were trading with India. They also brought back from China silks that had been carried overland and traded in the marketplaces of Arabia. Slaves from all nations were collected to be sold in the market. Blond slaves from Germany fetched the best prices. The Romans were so fascinated with blond hair that many of them began to wear blond wigs. Other plunder — gold in large quantities, money, and works of art — were sent back by the armies on campaign. From Africa came ivory, ostrich eggs, and the wild animals that were to be slaughtered in the arena for the delight of the Roman citizens. In return, out of Ostia went wine, olive oil, pottery, glassware, bronze goods, and military supplies. Pleasure yachts sailed from the harbor, carrying tourists. And there were unusual cargoes, too, ranging from fish sauce to prefabricated columns for use in the building projects of Herod the Great in Palestine.

PIRATES

Augustus knew that if trade was to expand, the ships that bustled in and out of Ostia and Italy's other ports needed the protection of a strong fleet. In the years before he came to power, pirates had been a threat. There were two kinds of piracy. The first was small scale and local. A man might assemble a crew of cutthroats, equip a small ship, and plunder any cargo vessels that came along. Sometimes four or five ships might join together to form a pirate fleet. In the early days Rome had little experience of war at sea and seamanship. Its legions were geared to fighting on land. During the wars with Carthage, the strongest sea power in the Mediterranean, they were forced to learn quickly. A Carthaginian ship was captured and copied by Roman craftsmen. Slowly the Romans began to master the new arts of sea warfare.

As a young man, Julius Caesar had been captured by such pirates. They demanded a huge ransom for him. Caesar did not seem at all concerned about the danger he faced. He told the pirates that the ransom they had set for such an important figure as himself was far too modest and offered them over double the amount. He laughed and joked with his captors and behaved more like their leader than their prisoner. He also promised them that as soon as he was freed he would raise a fleet and destroy them. This is exactly what he did. He confiscated their money and, on his own authority, crucified all of them.

The second form of piracy was on a much bigger scale. Pompey the Great, Caesar's rival, had cleared the Mediterranean of part-time pirates. Pompey's son, Sextus, took over his father's fleets and occupied Sicily. From there

A Roman merchant ship puts into Ostia with cargo from abroad that includes families destined to be sold as slaves.

43

A kitchen floor mosaic showing some favorite Roman seafoods.

By the time of the Battle of Actium, Agrippa's fleet had become so confident that the fight was over almost before it began. Cleopatra's ship scuttled back to Egypt. Antonius, on the flagship of his fleet, followed her. Octavian was left with his rival's fleet as well as his own — a total of some 700 ships. They were mostly triremes of Greek design. Octavian created three standing fleets, one stationed at Ravenna on Italy's northeast coast, another at Misenum just over 100 miles south of Rome. The third was based at Forum Julii, near Massilia (modern Marseilles). From there it controlled the coasts of Gaul and Spain.

The fleets were treated as auxiliary units and part of the army. They were commanded by cavalry officers who had trained as legionary tribunes and who were responsible directly to the emperor. The individual ships were commanded by Augustus' servants or even trusted slaves. The sailors were recruited mainly from Egypt and Dalmatia on the Adriatic. They had to sign up for twenty-six years and were granted Roman citizenship when their term of service was complete.

Many people assume that the triremes were rowed by slaves. Films like *Ben Hur* show banks of slaves chained to their oars, being flogged by bad tempered, brutal slave-masters. It is true that galleys used in Spain much closer to our own times — as recently as 300 years ago — were rowed in this way, but the Hollywood version is false. There is no evidence that slaves were ever used to row Roman ships. The oarsmen were paid soldiers, skilled seamen, very proud of their achievements.

Augustus almost certainly created smaller permanent fleets wherever he felt they were required. He kept fleets

he could hold Rome itself to ransom by capturing the enormous grain ships that came from Egypt. This was in the early days when Octavian and Antonius were supposed to be working together. After defeats at sea, Octavian put his fleets in the hands of Agrippa. Thanks to a new weapon called the harpax — a catapult that fired a grapnel and locked the vessels together — Agrippa's men could swarm aboard the enemy ship and fight as if they were on land. Octavian risked everything on a final sea battle. Sextus was defeated and fled to Antonius. He warned Antonius that Octavian was becoming too powerful and that one day he would turn on his former friend. Then Sextus claimed that his great experience of sea warfare could be useful in such a crisis. Antonius cut his head off.

A fast-food bar in Pompeii. The holes in the counter would have held jars of wine. Pompeii was rich in wine, oil and grain, and exported its surplus.

in Egypt and Syria and also set up river fleets on the Rhine and the Danube. In addition he permitted his trusted allies to build royal fleets that he could call upon when necessary. Herod the Great, as one might expect, formed his private fleet and based it at Caesarea — the new town and harbor that he named in honor of Augustus.

LIVING FROM THE SEA

A great many Roman citizens earned their money from the sea. There was work for fishermen who sold their catch on the dockside or in the city markets soon after it was caught, since it is difficult to keep fish fresh in hot weather. Some were also sold live from saltwater tanks. This method can still be seen today in the markets of Naples. Crabs, lobsters, shrimps, squid, and oysters were caught near the shore in traps and small nets or by divers. Farther out to sea, much bigger nets were used.

Boat building was a thriving industry. Barges for river transport, fishing vessels, and merchant sailing ships with deep holds were in demand. Sail-makers, rope-makers, ballast-loaders, and caulkers were all kept busy.

The wreckage of a Roman ship, photographed by divers on the Mediterranean seabed. The cargo consisted mainly of amphorae - vessels for wine and oil - and pottery.

The docks at Ostia bustled with life. Porters with carts and donkey trains moved back and forth between the huge warehouses and the ships. Smaller boats, barges, and rafts ferried goods upriver to the heart of Rome. Because so much wealth was transported, pilfering was common, and the docks had to employ their own police force.

The ships themselves were fairly fragile craft. They tended to stay close to shore and could not stand up to the rough weather that is common in the Mediterranean. For most of the winter, ships did not venture out of port, and even at more favorable times of year storms could spring up with alarming suddenness. Augustus himself was shipwrecked at least twice. Some years later St. Paul was shipwrecked on his way to Rome. His experience is described in the New Testament. Roman wrecks littered the coastlines of the empire. The ships that went down have long since rotted away, but modern divers often find row upon row of wine jars or even richer cargoes neatly stacked on the seabed just as they were packed many hundreds of years ago.

CHAPTER 9

Living in Rome

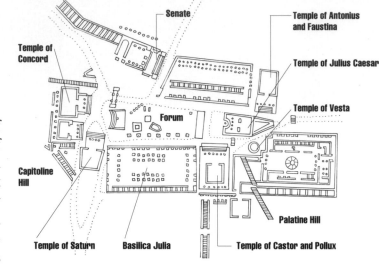

Senate

Temple of Antonius and Faustina

Temple of Concord

Temple of Julius Caesar

Temple of Vesta

Forum

Capitoline Hill

Palatine Hill

Temple of Saturn

Basilica Julia

Temple of Castor and Pollux

ABOVE: Map of the Roman Forum during Augustus' rule. RIGHT: A typical Roman street with apartment buildings. Except for the costumes and pottery utensils, such a scene might well have its counterpart today in the Trastevere district of Rome.

The boundaries of the ancient city of Rome had been marked by a priest plowing a furrow with a team of sacred oxen. Over the furrow the first walls had been built. By the time of Augustus, the original city had expanded to such an extent that it absorbed its neighboring towns such as Lavinium, Ostia, Veii, and Tibur. The line of the first furrow — the *pomerium* — had long ceased to represent the true boundaries of Rome. Augustus divided both the old and new parts of the city into fourteen districts, each governed by magistrates.

The old section of Rome contained the public buildings, gardens and parks, major temples, and the business center. The very rich owned villas in the countryside or beside the sea. There were a few splendid houses in the city, but most people were crammed into high-rise apartment buildings. Apart from the houses of the imperial family — and even Augustus' home was quite modest compared with those of some of his wealthy friends — rich and poor tended to live side by side wherever space was available.

APARTMENT BUILDINGS

Because space was so limited, rents were often very high. Landlords built taller and taller buildings in order to cram more people in. Concrete was of a low quality, and there was no steel to reinforce it. Each floor in a building of three or four floors had to be supported by heavy timberwork. Nor were there inspectors to ensure that construction was of a high, or even safe, standard. As a result, buildings often collapsed, killing all the people in them. It was said of Crassus, a friend of Julius Caesar, that he often arrived on the scene of a newly collapsed apartment building, offered the owner a small cash payment for the smoldering ruin, and then erected a higher building, charging double the rent. Augustus passed a law prohibiting buildings higher than 60-65 feet. But many landlords ignored it.

There were two main kinds of apartment buildings. The more expensive type presented solid walls to the street. All the doors and windows opened onto a central courtyard. The upper stories had projecting balconies and wooden stairs. The owner might occupy the entire ground floor or rent it to a rich family. The second floor contained apartments with two or three rooms. Everything — shopping, water, laundry — had to be carried up several flights of stairs. People made the reverse journey with chamber pots and commodes. So the higher you climbed, the worse was the accommodation. The cheapest one-room apartments were usually on the top floor.

ABOVE: *A Roman bakery. Then, as now, products included a tempting range of bread loaves, rolls, cakes, and pies.*
RIGHT CENTER: *An elaborately carved table from Pompeii.*
RIGHT: *An aristocrat entertains his guests at dinner.*

The less expensive type of apartment building followed the same general plan, but the doors and windows opened onto the street. The balconies on the upper floors projected out over the street. The occupants, perhaps remembering happier times in the countryside, covered these balconies with climbing plants, shrubs, pots of flowers, and window boxes. Water had to be carried up for these, too, and doubtless the contents of many a chamber pot were emptied into a pot of flowers. The ground floor was occupied by shops, bars, or workshops.

FURNITURE AND TABLEWARE

There was not much furniture in the average apartment. Most people slept on a wooden-frame bed, which was used as a couch during the day. The rich slept in beds made of expensive woods that had bronze or silver feet. Married couples had double beds. Mattresses rested on wooden grids or rope webbing. They often contained bedbugs. Simple folding chairs were not unknown, but benches and stools were more common. Some richer families had chests or lockable strongboxes in which they kept money, valuables, and clothes. Cupboards were very rare. The rich spent large amounts of money on the decoration of their houses, works of art, and elaborate gardens.

Adults ate reclining on couches, usually in pairs, the food being served on low tables. Only children and slaves sat down to eat. The rich ate from silver plates and drank from decorated silver

Women drawing water from a street well. The city's water was supplied by the aqueducts from the hills outside Rome.

cups. Most people used glazed red pottery called Samian-ware, which was not very expensive and easy to clean. As nobody discovered anything more suitable, it was used for centuries. People are still using similar products today. Samian-ware plates, cups, and wine jugs were exported all over the then-known world.

COOKING AND BAKING

Most Romans ate in the thousands of snack bars that could be found in all parts of the city. Not all houses had kitchens. At home, food was cooked on an iron tripod placed over a flat raised surface on which a charcoal fire burned. Underneath was a brick arch used for storing firewood and charcoal. There was also a stone sink with no drain. Some houses in the Greek islands still have identical cooking arrangements even today. Pans were generally made of bronze, but because this sometimes gave certain foods an unpleasant taste, the rich had theirs coated with silver. Wooden spoons were used for cooking. Knives were very similar to those used today but were not made of stainless-steel and needed constant sharpening. Terracotta and glass jars were used for storage, but glass was very expensive.

Bread, the most important item in the Roman diet, was bought at a bakery. Ovens were just like modern Italian pizza ovens — those, at any rate, which have not been converted to gas or electricity. Burning wood was placed in the oven until the bricks lining the walls became very hot. Then the fire was scraped out and the dough — or pizza — was placed on the oven bottom, using a thin wooden paddle. The opening was sealed by a wooden door until the bread was cooked. Roman bakers also sold a wide range of cakes, pies, and snacks.

In Augustus' time, the government supplemented the diets of nearly one-third of Rome's population. There were free distributions of corn or bread and even wine.

HEATING AND LIGHTING

An oil-burning candelabra from Pompeii.

Some people think that all Roman houses had central heating. This is not true. In most homes the only heating came from small charcoal-burning braziers. As for illumination, candles were used, but oil lamps were the main source of light. These lamps ranged from the simple terracotta type to elaborate works of art in bronze or silver. There was no glass in windows. They were fitted with heavy wooden shutters that had to be opened or closed. In winter, when it was too cold to have the shutters open, lamps provided the only lighting — and dozens of them were needed to illuminate the smallest of rooms.

HYGIENE

Rome boasted a truly magnificent sewage system and a few of the ground floor apartments of the rich sometimes had toilets connected to them. Unfortunately, the other apartments were not so well equipped. Nor did the sewers extend to all parts of the city. Some private toilets and public latrines merely emptied into a cess trench which was often situated in the heart of a heavily populated area and leaked out onto the street or the ground floors of nearby houses. But there were a great number of public toilets. The seats formed a semicircle or a rectangle. Water from one of the aqueducts flowed under the seats to carry the ordure to the sewers. The toilet thus became a meeting place where the Roman citizen could, for a small fee, sit and chat with his friends, discuss politics, or exchange dinner invitations.

There was no charge for the use of the urinals outside the fullers' shops. Fulling is part of the cloth-making process, for which large quantities of urine were essential. Fullers placed large jars outside their shops in which passers-by were encouraged to urinate. About fifty-five years after Augustus died, the emperor Vespasian taxed the fullers on the public collection of urine. They were not amused.

ROADS AND STREETS

Only two streets in Rome could be considered worthy of the name: the Via Sacra and the Via Nova — the Sacred Way and New Street. The rest were often narrow, filthy, muddy tracks, frequently choked with garbage. Julius Caesar ordered all landlords to keep the streets around their property clean, but most ignored him. Where there were pavements, shopkeepers covered them with stalls, bar owners with benches, schoolteachers with pupils. Complaints about filthy streets have always been a favorite theme in Roman prose and poetry.

There was no street lighting, and after sundown, the city was enveloped in profound darkness. On festival days the citizens would illuminate their city with torches, bonfires, and

Diagram of a typical Roman house from Pompeii.

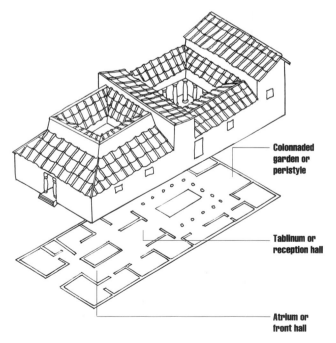

Colonnaded garden or peristyle

Tablinum or reception hall

Atrium or front hall

lanterns. On other nights they stayed at home, unless forced to do otherwise. Then they had to splash through the mud and filth, carrying a torch or following a slave bearing one. On the night of Julius Caesar's assassination, angry Roman mobs lit bonfires. The conspirators took advantage of the extra light to visit one another and plot their next moves. Night held the added danger of being killed, either by robbers or by traffic.

Julius Caesar passed a law, and Augustus confirmed it, that no traffic was allowed in the center of Rome during the day. The only exceptions were the chariots of people celebrating a triumph, the carriages of the Vestal Virgins, others that were required in public processions, and the carts of building material merchants — doubtless off to supply constructors of collapsed apartment buildings. As a result, when night fell, the darkened streets were crowded with carts of merchandise, cattle going to market, people moving from one house to another, farm-

ABOVE: Given the flimsy wooden structures and the overcrowded living conditions, fires often spread rapidly through the poorer areas of the city.
BELOW: View of a Pompeii street, with Mount Vesuvius in the background.

ers bringing food, oil and wine, cess trench emptiers, soldiers transporting military supplies, and animal cages on their way to the circus. The noise and confusion was unbearable. People visiting Rome for the first time wondered how the Romans slept through it all. There was just no answer to the problem. People crammed the streets during the day, and if other traffic had been permitted, Rome would have ground to a standstill. Many cities today experience similar problems.

THE FIRE BRIGADE

If a house did not collapse, it was likely to burn down. Open cooking fires and oil lamps meant a constant danger of fire. In A.D. 6 Augustus established a fire brigade called the *Cohortes Vigilum*. There were plenty of public fountains, so small fires, if caught in time, could be extinguished with buckets of water. Where a fire had taken hold, the only way to try to contain it was to pull the building down or prevent it from spreading by demolishing the neighboring buildings.

A PUBLIC LIFE

One could be forgiven for thinking that life in Rome was unbearable for all but the very rich, and that there were few home comforts. The fact is that Roman citizens spent very little time at home. They worked in public, enjoyed themselves in public at festivals and circuses, worshiped the gods in public, bathed in public, and, as we have seen, even relieved themselves in public.

Augustus, and the emperors who followed him, knew that, if the citizens of Rome were to be kept happy, it was their public life that would have to be provided for. This is why Rome had free bread, public shows and games, magnificent temples and public buildings, and amazing sewers and aqueducts. We must also remember that during the reign of Augustus, more than 155 days in each year were public holidays.

CHAPTER 10

Living in the Countryside

People who are forced to spend most of their lives in towns often have very romantic ideas about life in the country. Originally all Romans had been farmers. When they came to live in the city, they chose to remember only the good things about those early days.

Augustus himself was no exception. He had spent much of his childhood on his stepfather's estate at Vellitrae, some 25 miles south of Rome. He liked people to think of him as a countryman, with a countryman's qualities and values — simplicity, honesty, industry, and common sense.

For most of the people who lived on the land — poor farmers or slaves — the daily round was one of backbreaking work. The rich, who lived in the city, owned farmland throughout Italy. Their farms were worked by slave labor. A wealthy family would build and boast of villas in the countryside or at the seaside in much the same way as rich city dwellers nowadays speak proudly of their "little place in the country." Some of these villas were more like palaces or even small towns than farms. Their owners retreated to them for holidays or when they happened to be out of favor at court. Many of them enjoyed hunting, which was as much a passion with the Romans of Augustus' time as it is with Italians today, except that game was then far more plentiful. Roman villas, however, were seldom just holiday homes. Most of them were expected to be run as profitable businesses.

For the vast majority of people, however, life in the country was very hard work. Poorer farmers toiled from dawn to dusk and lived with their families and a few slaves. They had to exist on what they produced themselves, and when the weather was bad and harvests were poor, they often found themselves near starvation.

The main crops grown in Italy were wheat, grapes, and olives. However, the land could not produce enough wheat to feed the entire population, and large quantities had to be imported, mainly from Sicily, Africa, and Augustus' private province of Egypt. Goats and cattle were kept for meat, milk, and hides; sheep for milk and wool.

Slaves harvesting corn and grapes on the land of a wealthy farmer. Wine, olive oil, and cereals were among the many products that provided lucrative income for the rich and fed the citizens of Rome.

THE OLD GODS

Farmers in the age of Augustus were much closer to the land than the city dwellers in more ways than the obvious. In the town, the new gods were worshiped in magnificent temples. In the countryside, older beliefs in gods who were nearer to the forces of nature still survived. Many of the city's religious festivals had their origins in long-forgotten fertility rites. Varro, a writer of the time who had a great deal to say about agriculture, described the deities who control nature.

Jupiter is the sky, Tellus Mater the earth mother. Sol and Luna, the sun and moon, rule seedtime and harvest. Liber and Ceres look after wine and crops. Robigus protects plants from disease, and Flora makes flowers grow. Minerva cares for olive groves and Venus for gardens. Nymphs water the crops, and Bonus Eventus rewards the farmer's hard work. Faunus looks after flocks, and in the wild forests lives Silvanus — a dangerous spirit, to be treated with the greatest respect.

Diana, goddess of hunting and moonlight, was one of the oldest Italian deities. She lived in the streams and groves of the forest. She was also a spirit not to be tangled with. Legend said that Actaeon, a young huntsman, watched Diana bathing by moonlight. In revenge, the goddess

The ritual sacrifice of the lamb formed the climax of Ambarvalia, the rural festival of blessing the crops.

turned the youth into a stag. Actaeon was promptly ripped to pieces by his own hounds.

The oldest and most powerful of the old agricultural gods was Saturn, the sower. All farmers were said to be descended from him. While he ruled the heavens and earth, everybody lived in peace with one another, and the harvest never failed. People called this "The Golden Age".

COUNTRY FESTIVALS

Saturn gave his name to a twelve-day winter feast, Saturnalia, which reached its climax on the twenty-fifth of December. The winter solstice is the year's shortest day and longest night. As the new year began, Romans decorated their houses with holly, exchanged gifts, and sometimes set free faithful and hard working slaves. There were all sorts of fun and games. Masters waited on their servants, bonfires were lit, and feasting went on right through the hours

Romulus and Remus, as depicted in this old etching, remained a popular theme in Roman mythology down to modern times.

of darkness. When Christianity became the accepted religion of the Roman Empire, Saturnalia was replaced by Christmas.

For the annual feast of Ambarvalia, a magic circle was drawn around the farm to protect its occupants from evil. The father of the house, together with his family and slaves, dressed in clean white clothes and crowned with olive wreaths, would lead a white lamb around the boundary of the estate. Afterward prayers were offered, the lamb was sacrificed, and the remainder of the day and night was spent eating and drinking.

The feast of Lupercalia was celebrated in Rome during February. Nobody could remember much about its origins. As its name suggests, it may have been a religious ceremony designed to protect the flocks from wolves, or it may have had something to do with Pluto, god of the underworld, who was often shown with a wolf mask. Pluto represented the deadness of winter. Legend had it that he carried off Proserpina, the daughter of Ceres, goddess of crops and fruitfulness. For six months Proserpina stayed with Pluto in the underworld, and nothing would grow. Her return to earth was celebrated as the return of spring. In Rome, at the time of Augustus, naked boys, known as wolf boys, would rush around the city striking women with wolf-skin thongs. This was supposed to make women fertile and protect the city from evil.

CHAPTER 11

Turning Bricks to Marble

Great building projects are often a favorite venture of powerful rulers. It is as if they wish to leave a record of their success in stone. They hope their achievements will be remembered forever. The dictators Adolf Hitler and Benito Mussolini were both obsessed with buildings on a massive scale. Nearer our own time, Nicolae Ceausescu of Romania and Saddam Hussein of Iraq spent fortunes that their countries could ill afford on vast palaces. Saddam hoped to rebuild the splendors of Babylon, the ancient capital of Iraq. One problem is that if these powerful people fall from popularity, their buildings tend to suffer. Their enemies take great delight in blowing these signs of former power into little bits.

A CITY TO ADMIRE

One of Augustus' favorite boasts was that he had found Rome a city of brick and left it a city of marble. Once he had made himself master of the known world, he began to spend a great deal of his time on building projects.

Augustus' principal helper in his building activities was his friend Agrippa, who had been at the emperor's side since his schooldays. He had proved himself as Augustus' best general. After Actium, Agrippa was to discover new talents. He became the city's chief planner, engineer, and even its building contractor.

AQUEDUCTS AND SEWERS

Agrippa knew that a good supply of pure water was essential for the well-being of all the citizens. Rome's water came by way of a series of

ABOVE: Arcade of an ancient Roman aqueduct the Aqua Anio Nonus Roma Vecchia.
BELOW: Channel of the same aqueduct, showing clearly how the water was conducted.

aqueducts from the hills around the city. The Aqua Claudia had been built in 312 B.C. As the population grew, more water was needed. The Aqua Vetus was built in 272 B.C., followed in 140 B.C. by the Aqua Marcia, and in 125 B.C. by the Aqua Tepula. However, Agrippa found that these old aqueducts could not meet Rome's requirements of this time and were in need of urgent repair. In 33 B.C. he opened the Aqua Julia, which brought a new supply of water from the Alban hills, southeast of Rome. He also employed a large task force of slaves to repair

ABOVE: The completed Cloaca Maxima, one of Rome's principal sewers, was wide enough to permit Agrippa to drive his chariot through it.
LEFT: Mouth of the Cloaca Maxima today, through which flowed tons of Roman sewage.

and maintain the old aqueducts, reservoirs, and drains. When he died, Agrippa left the slaves in his will to Augustus, who gave them to the city. It is strange to think of buying a plumber or two rather than telephoning for one.

Some of the water found its way into the houses of the rich. A private supply was very expensive. Most of it went to public drinking

CONCRETE AND MARBLE

The Romans had known how to make concrete long before the time of Augustus. But the quality of concrete had been improving all the time. Architects started to experiment with domed concrete roofs and found they could cover larger and larger areas. The scale of buildings began to increase and continued to do so. The modern town of Split in Yugoslavia is built inside the remains of the palace of the later emperor, Diocletian.

Most of Augustus' great buildings were made of kiln-baked bricks and concrete. But they were faced with marble. Near Luna in northern Italy were the Carrara marble quarries, which produced some of the finest white marble in the world. Augustus loved white marble. It is easy to cut and carve, and it looks wonderfully clean, cool, and crisp. The quarries became one of the major industries in Italy as the demand from Rome grew and grew. Marble of different colors was imported from all over the ancient world — yellow from Africa, pink, green, and blue from Greece and Asia Minor (modern Turkey) being the most popular.

fountains, baths, gardens, and latrines. Some people tried to cheat. They would make holes in the lead piping of the aqueducts, connect their own pipes, and channel water illegally into their homes. Fines for those who were caught were very severe.

Agrippa was very proud of the work he did building new sewers and repairing old ones. The Cloaca Maxima, flushed with water from the new aqueducts, was extended and widened by him. Agrippa took great delight in driving up and down the sewer in a chariot. It was almost as if he was celebrating a triumph. And in a way he was.

One serious problem faced Augustus and Agrippa when they first set out on their program of building. Few Roman builders knew how to work in marble. Augustus solved the difficulty by employing a vast work force of Greek craftsmen. They brought with them Greek ways of doing things. Augustus' buildings combined a Roman expertise in engineering with a Greek expertise in making things look beautiful.

STATUES

There were many statues of Augustus in Rome. Others were sent hundreds, even thousands, of miles to all corners of the empire. It was good for people in remote parts of the ancient world to know what the person who controlled their lives looked like. Portraits on coins did not tell nearly as much about the emperor as did his statues. Augustus was always shown as a handsome, dignified, purposeful leader. The citizens of Rome and the inhabitants of Rome's far-flung empire could have confidence in such a fine figure.

It was not only the highest in the land who had statues made of themselves. Anybody, usually for reasons of vanity, could do so. The rich Roman could go to the sculptor, choose a body in a suitable pose, then have his own head sculpted and attached.

EPILOGUE

In A.D. 14, when he was seventy-five years old, Augustus took a holiday on the island of Capri. He was returning to Rome on the same road he had traveled as a boy of eighteen, when he had decided to claim Julius Caesar's legacy. When he reached the villa at Nola that his family had owned for generations, he fell ill. On a camp bed, in the room where his father had died, Augustus spent his last hours. The body was taken to Rome and cremated with great ceremony. The Senate decreed that Augustus had become a god.

Perhaps Augustus' greatest regret was that he had left no male heir of his own family to succeed him. His daughter by his first marriage had given him grandchildren. All but one of his grandsons had died. Agrippa Posthumus, the remaining boy, was said to be insane and was secretly put to death a few days after Augustus himself died. Power then passed to his stepson, Tiberius, the son of Augustus' wife Livia by her first marriage.

Augustus had lived a long life in a position of total power. He ruled fairly and well. There is a saying that "absolute power corrupts absolutely." This was certainly true of many of the emperors who followed Augustus — Caligula, Nero, and Domitian were brutal, incompetent, and eventually insane. Augustus was the exception to the rule. He was stubborn and single-minded, but he always put the interests of his country before everything else. He covered

Rome's public buildings in pure white marble: his own house was very simple. He liked good plain food. He liked plain speaking. He hated flattery and expected everybody to treat him as an equal. He hated waste and luxury. His wife and family made all his clothes. He enjoyed being surrounded by his family. The Senate voted him many honors. Perhaps the one of which Augustus was proudest was "Father of His Country."

Statue of the emperor Augustus as a young man.

Glossary

AFRICA A small Roman province on the coast, west of Egypt. It provided grain for the empire.

ALEXANDER THE GREAT A Macedonian king who, by the age of twenty-six, had built an empire that extended from Greece to modern-day Pakistan. This formed a large part of the later Roman Empire.

AMBARVALIA A Roman festival of blessing the crops.

CARTHAGE A city founded by the Phoenicians in North Africa. Carthage established an empire that became a rival to early Rome. Rome and Carthage fought two great wars. Under their general, Hannibal, the Carthaginians repeatedly defeated the Roman legions and threatened Rome itself. Carthage was eventually crushed and the city destroyed, leaving Rome the most powerful force in the world.

CELTS A group of warlike tribes, skilled in iron work, that spread from the Black Sea over most of eastern and western Europe. They were a threat to the early Romans but were finally subjected. Their descendants still live in many parts of Europe.

COHORT A division of the Roman army.

CONSULS Rome's chief magistrates and commanders of its armies. After expelling its kings, Rome elected two consuls annually, thus ensuring that neither official became too powerful.

FORUM (pl. Fora) Rome's central social and business district, originally a marketplace, like the Agora in Athens. The emperors built various fora, adorning them with covered walks, temples, and public buildings.

INCENSE Natural perfumes, gums, and resins burned on altars to please the gods and perhaps to hide the less attractive aroma of burning flesh.

LEGION A division of the Roman army containing between 6,000 and 8,000 soldiers.

LUPERCALIA A Roman festival when naked boys ran around the streets of Rome hitting women with thongs made of wolf hide, which was thought to make them become pregnant.

MAGISTRATE A Roman officer of the law.

MESS A place where soldiers eat together, or the food they eat.

PALATINE HILL The city of Rome sprawls over seven hills. It is probable that the Palatine was the first one (chosen, according to legend, by Romulus, and settled by the tribe that would become Romans). The emperors built their homes on the Palatine.

PHARAOH The ruler of Egypt, supposed to be a god in heaven and a king on earth. When Alexander the Great conquered Egypt, he became its pharaoh. So did the Greek family that ruled there after him, including Cleopatra, who in terms of Egyptian symbol and ritual was a man. There were no female pharaohs.

PRECINCT Originally, in the days when people were close to the gods of nature, a sacred grove around a shrine or temple dedicated to a god or a divine hero. Later, a public park.

SARCOPHAGUS A stone box containing a dead body.

SOLOMON'S TEMPLE In Jerusalem, the most sacred site for Jews; it contained the sanctuary where God had his earthly throne room. Herod the Great rebuilt it in great splendor, but six years after its opening it was destroyed by the Roman general, and later emperor, Titus.

TRIREME A warship rowed by three banks of oars.

VICTIM An animal without blemish sacrificed to the gods.

Index